THE *Bride's* THANK-YOU NOTE HANDBOOK

Marilyn Werner

A FIRESIDE BOOK
Published by Simon & Schuster

NEW YORK   LONDON   TORONTO   SYDNEY

Fireside
A Division of Simon & Schuster, Inc.
1230 Avenue of the Americas
New York, NY 10020

This Fireside trade paperback edition June 2010

FIRESIDE and colophon are registered trademarks of Simon & Schuster, Inc.

For information about special discounts for bulk purchases,
please contact Simon & Schuster Special Sales at 1-866-506-1949
or business@simonandschuster.com.

The Simon & Schuster Speakers Bureau can bring authors to your live event.
For more information or to book an event contact
the Simon & Schuster Speakers Bureau at 1-866-248-3049
or visit our website at www.simonspeakers.com.

Manufactured in the United States of America

1   3   5   7   9   10   8   6   4   2

Library of Congress Cataloging-in-Publication Data
Werner, Marilyn.
The bride's thank-you note handbook.
p.   cm.
"A Fireside book."
Rev. Fireside ed.
1. Thank-you notes 2. Wedding etiquette. I. Title.
BJ2065.T53 W47 1985
395'.22—dc19   85-14180

ISBN 978-1-4391-8926-9
ISBN 978-1-4391-9031-9 (ebook)

*Dedicated to those who have always given
their support, encouragement, and love—
Stacy Lynn and Michael Chamis*

Contents

Introduction

Books dealing with wedding etiquette correctly point out that courtesy requires the bride to promptly acknowledge all gifts with a handwritten thank-you note. Unfortunately, after presenting this piece of advice, most books proceed to other subjects leaving the bride without instructions on how to compose her notes and what to include in them. *The Bride's Thank-you Note Handbook* answers these questions.

This book contains an extensive collection of sample thank-you notes which you, the bride, may adapt to your own needs. The models, arranged alphabetically by gift, include almost every type of present that you are likely to receive. Sometimes you may choose to copy a model letter word for word; other times you may want to change a few words or add others. In any case, your job will be considerably simplified and, with the time you save from this arduous task, you will be able to engage in other more delightful pursuits—namely, the enjoyment of your own wedding and honeymoon.

There are so many good options for saying thanks. Of course, there are preprinted thank-you cards you can buy; all you need to do is sign them. This time-saving method is admittedly appealing. However, because preprinted thank-you cards do not reflect your personal appreciation, or demonstrate adequate effort, they really are unacceptable.

The phone provides you with another quick and easy way to say thanks. How tempting! Sometimes you don't even need to place the call—the call comes to you. This call can come for many different reasons, such as the gift giver calling to see if you have received the gift, had a chance to use it, or simply to see if you liked the selection. He or she could even be calling to wait for you say thank you. It is certainly appropriate to express your appreciation—but that is no substitute for following up with a written thank-you note.

Today, there are so many high-tech ways to communicate—e-mail, instant messaging, social networking sites like Facebook or MySpace, chat rooms, and even webcams where you can see each other face-to-face. It's hard not to take the path of least resistance. With all the preparation of a wedding behind you, it's only natural to want to relax and not have to deal with more details, but the traditional handwritten thank-you note remains accepted—and expected. There is no substitute for showing that you appreciate the time, money, and effort that was spent to select a gift or to provide help with your wedding activities that made your wedding day so special. So read on and learn dozens of easy, painless ways to send your heartfelt regards to your family and friends.

Chapter One

GETTING STARTED

An Efficient Routine

Try to establish some kind of routine for writing your thank-you notes. Set aside a specific time each day for this purpose, and within that period try to write at least four or five so they don't pile up.

Reserve a particular place to write your thank-you notes; a place where you are not apt to be disturbed or distracted. Keep your gift cards, stationery, gift lists, pen, dictionary, and stamps at that spot.

The Gift Cards

Save the gift cards that are enclosed with the gifts. After you have read them keep them together in a box or bound securely with a rubber band. When you write your notes, refer to these gift cards, for they often express lovely and touching sentiments that are as worthy of acknowledgment as the gifts themselves.

The Stationery

Thank-you notes should always be handwritten on good quality sta-tionery. Plain folded note paper in white or ecru is most popular, but pastel shades, with simple borders or lined envelopes, are acceptable. The bride's monogram, either engraved or printed, may be used for notes written after the wedding date. The appearance of your thank-you note is important, so use your best handwriting. Leave some margin on both sides of the paper, and see to it that there is as much blank space at the top of the paper as there is at the bottom. If the note is badly smudged or if you have crossed out a word, it is better to rewrite the note.

When you have finished your note, read it aloud to make sure that you have not omitted or misspelled any words. This is the surest way of catching and correcting any careless errors.

When mailing your thank-you notes, insert the note in the enve-lope so that when it is removed the writing will be right side up and can be read without inverting the paper. Moisten, do not tuck in, the flap of the envelope.

The Structure of a Thank-You Note

A thank-you note consists of four parts: a *salutation*, a *body*, a *compli-mentary closing*, and a *signature*. The date is included above the saluta-tion in the upper right-hand corner of the paper.

The *salutation* usually begins with "Dear" and always ends with a comma (not a colon). When the gift is sent by a married couple the thank-you note may be addressed to either "Mr. and Mrs." or to the wife only. In the latter case, however, you should make sure to men-tion the husband within the body of the note.

You may wonder how to address the groom's relatives, some of whom you may not even have met. Although you may feel inclined to address them as Mr. and Mrs., you should remember that they are now (or are going to be) your relatives too. They should, therefore, be addressed, for instance, as Aunt and Uncle. In most cases, you will probably see them at some later date and call them Aunt and Uncle anyhow.

The *body* is the main portion of the note, in which you will convey your thanks. Try to make your note as personal and individual as possible. You can do this by mentioning the gift by name and by saying something about its usefulness or appearance. If the gift is a check, describe how you have used it (or plan to use it) or what you have purchased with it. Sometimes, too, you will want to say something to the effect that you are looking forward to seeing the people in your new home, where the gift they have given you will occupy a very special place.

Do not confuse enthusiasm with overeffusiveness, or warm feeling with oversentimentality. Expressions like "heartfelt thanks," "forever and ever," "the most tremendous," and "in seventh heaven" should be avoided. Warmth of feeling and enthusiasm can be expressed in fresher and usually more restrained ways.

Note the differences in the following three notes. The last one is clearly the best because it is the warmest and most personal.

NOT ACCEPTABLE

Dear Janis and Dave,

Thank you so much for your beautiful gift. We appreciate it.

Love,
Marilyn

ACCEPTABLE

> *Dear Janis and Dave,*
>
> *Thank you so much for your beautiful linen set. We will be the envy of all our friends when we invite them to dinner. We appreciate it very much.*
>
> *Love,*
> *Marilyn*

PERFECT

> *Dear Janis and Dave,*
>
> *Thank you so much for your linen set. It is so beautiful that we plan to use it only on special occasions, one of which will be an evening with you—we hope in the near future.*
>
> *Love,*
> *Marilyn*

The *complimentary closing* will depend on your relationship with the people to whom you are writing. With close friends and relatives, "love," "fondly," "affectionately" are quite acceptable. When the ties are not so close, you might choose to close with "sincerely" or "gratefully." "Sincerely yours" and "yours truly" are a bit too formal.

The *signature* consists of the bride's name only, never that of both the bride and the groom. If your note is addressed to people who have always known you by your first name, sign your first name only. To people who do not know you well, sign with your maiden name (e.g., Marilyn Maiden Name) before the wedding and with your married name (e. g., Marilyn Married Name) after the wedding. In cases where a more explicit identification is necessary, you may use your maiden and married names (e. g., Marilyn [Maiden] Married Name), but only after the wedding.

A sample thank-you note, with each part labeled, follows:

June 16, 20—(1)

Dear Mrs. Jones, (2)

Both you and Mr. Jones have been so marvelous to us during these last hectic months that we don't know how to thank you. Now, with the arrival of your magnificent silver fruit bowl, we are doubly indebted to you. Thank you so very much for everything. (3)

Fondly, (4)
Marilyn (5)

---

1. Date
2. Salutation
3. Body
4. Complimentary closing
5. Signature

The Gift Acknowledgment

Make every effort to write your thank-you note as soon as possible after receiving the gift. If, however, you anticipate a long delay, either because of the number of gifts that you have received or because of the myriad details associated with the wedding, you may do one of two things: First, you may acknowledge the gift verbally by calling to thank the person who has given it to you or by thanking him in person. If the giver is your fiancé's (or husband's) friend, your fiancé may convey your thanks, adding that you plan to send a note in the near future. If the person is a friend of your parents or in-laws, you may say that you have received the gift and intend to send a personal note shortly. Second, you may acknowledge the receipt of the gift by sending out an engraved card acknowledging that you have received the gift and plan to write a personal thank-you note in the near future. The disadvantage is that this is an extra expense. A few short lines at the outset can save lots of time and effort in the end.

GIFT LIST FOR GROOM'S SIDE

Name	Address	Gift
Mary Bently	20 Stone Dr. Orange, NJ	hand mixer
Phoebe Richards	10 E. 19 St. New York, NY	nightgown
Mr. and Mrs. S. Harding	14 S. Lake Dr. Scarsdale, NY	glass fruit bowl
Mr. and Mrs. Bart Lions	12 W. 78 St. New York, NY	stacking tables
Mr. and Mrs. T. Howell	6 Hyde St. Chicago, IL	silver tray
Mr. and Mrs. Jack Cloud	6 Belmont Dr. Los Angeles, CA	$50.00 gift certificate
Mr. and Mrs. John Stone	34 Olive St. Bronx, NY	casserole dish
Edward Thompson	158 N. Glen Rd. Belmont, NY	toaster

> *Miss Maiden Name*
>
> *or*
>
> *Mrs. Married Name*
> *acknowledges that she has received*
> *your gift and will write you a note*
> *of thanks as soon as she is able.*

The Gift Lists

Don't trust to your memory to help you keep track of all the gifts you have received and the people who have given them to you. Before you know it, you'll be playing the frustrating and time-consuming game called "Who gave me what?"

The surest way to remember who gave you what is to keep lists.

(Copy to be given to mother-in-law)

Occasion Received	Gift Arrived	Gift Acknowledged	Where Bought
shower (Joyce's)	5/26	5/28	Bed Bath & Beyond
shower (Barbara's)	5/26	5/28	Saks
engagement (Aunt Em's)	6/3	6/7	Bloomingdale's
engagement	6/12	6/15	Crate & Barrel
wedding	6/20	6/22	Saks
wedding	6/22	6/25	Tiffany
wedding	6/23	6/28	Macy's
wedding	6/28	7/3	Macy's

They should be kept in a notebook or on a pad, not on little scraps of paper that are easily lost. The first list will be for gifts received from your side of the family. The second list is for gifts received from the groom's side. When this list has been completed, your mother-in-law will appreciate a copy so she will know what gifts you have received from her friends and family. She may use this list (as you may too) as a reference if she has to send a gift in the future.

The list may be quite simple, consisting of three columns:

1. Sender's name
2. Sender's address
3. Gift

If you choose a more elaborate list (see pages 6–7), you may add:

4. Occasion gift given (this will remind you whether it was for a party, shower, engagement party, or the wedding)
5. Date gift received (this will enable you to thank people in the order the gifts arrive)
6. Gift acknowledged (this will be your assurance that you did indeed send a thank-you note)
7. Store where gift purchased (this information will be necessary if you want to return or exchange the gift)

A Word to the Wise

A written thank-you note does not pledge you to a conspiracy of silence when you see the people who have given you a gift. You and the groom should thank the people in person when you see them. If they are guests at your home, try to use their gift or display it.

Chapter Two

MODEL
THANK-YOU NOTES
FOR TYPICAL GIFTS

This chapter contains model thank-you notes for the gifts the bride and groom are most likely to receive. The sample notes have been listed alphabetically according to the gift. If the present you have received is listed, you may decide to use the corresponding note either in its entirety or in abbreviated form. If, however, the gift you have received is not specified, do not despair. From the model notes you will be able to select ideas and phrases that you can use in your own thank-you notes.

Airplane Tickets

Dear Joanne and John,

I didn't intend my telephone call to substitute for a written thank-you. However, we were so excited when we received the airplane tickets that I just had to rush to the phone. We had not yet finalized our honeymoon plans and your generous gift will now make our dream trip a reality! Thank you and aloha.

Love,
Marilyn

Art

Dear Mr. and Mrs. Laird,

Words can't describe our reaction to your exquisite painting. Its beauty speaks for itself. We hope that the art world won't feel deprived because the painting is now hanging in our apartment instead of being on display in a public gallery. Our sincerest thanks.

Fondly,
Marilyn

Bar Accessories

Dear Dee and Bob,

I predict that your bar accessories will make us the most popular host and hostess in town. We ask, though, for one final wedding favor—please plan to set aside an evening when we return from our honeymoon to join us for cocktails. Of course they'll be stirred, strained, and poured with your wonderful bar gifts. Our thanks to you both.

Affectionately,
Marilyn

Bathroom Accessories

Dear Aunt Martha,

Your bathroom accessories have made all the difference in our new apartment. Our bathroom was an afterthought with nothing coordinated. Now with the matching tissue box, soap dish, toothbrush holder, wastebasket, and matching shower curtain, our bathroom has taken on its own importance. We really appreciate your thoughtful gift.

Love,
Marilyn

Bedspread

Dear Terry and Kirby,

The bedspread is just beautiful. There is one problem, though—
not all of our guests will get to see it. Too bad beds don't belong
in the living room. Thank you for a lovely gift.

Love,
Marilyn

Blanket

Dear Nancy and Al,

You don't know how much your electric blanket is appreciated.
I've just discovered that George likes to sleep with the windows
wide-open! How I was dreading the onset of winter, with the
possibility of being frozen in my sleep. Your gift will save me
from such a sensational end. My warmest thanks to you.

Love,
Marilyn

Book Light

Dear Mr. and Mrs. Morris,

Thank you for your unusual and useful gift. Since I love few things better than reading myself to sleep with a good mystery, while George is a member of the early to bed, early-to-rise school, it will certainly come in handy! Every time I break the spine on a new thriller I will remember your thoughtfulness.

Sincerely,
Marilyn Werner

Bowl

Dear Mr. and Mrs. Blake,

The fruit bowl is so very beautiful that I plan to use it whenever I entertain. With so many friends watching their weight, your beautiful bowl will make serving fruit an enticing option. Thank you very much.

Fondly,
Marilyn

Camera

Dear Mr. and Mrs. Milland,

George and I want to thank you very much for the camera. Until its arrival, we didn't know how we were going to record our honeymoon. Your gift has solved the problem and completely thrilled us both. George is impressed with all its features, and I love the idea of simply pushing a button and letting the camera do all the work.

Sincerely,
Marilyn

Candelabrum

Dear Mr. and Mrs. Kent,

Thank you so much for the elegant candelabrum. With such fine craftsmanship it could easily grace any of the old-world palaces of Vienna or Paris. Needless to say, it will occupy a very exalted position at the Werner residence on Magnolia Street.

Gratefully,
Marilyn Werner

Candy Dish

Dear Alice,

Judging from the compliments I've received on your lovely candy dish, it won't be long now before the stores are all sold out of this perfect gift. Thank you ever so much for catering to my sweet tooth.

Affectionately,
Marilyn

Can Opener

Dear Phyllis,

You can't imagine how thrilled I am with my new electric can opener. I anticipate there will be many evenings when it will be put to emergency use after I have burned our dinner. Your practical gift is very much appreciated.

Love,
Marilyn

Casserole Dish

Dear Carol and Marv,

*I truly believe it is the prettiest casserole dish I've ever seen.
With a dish like this it's almost a crime not to serve a casserole
every night of the week. In fact, I've already started to look for
new casserole recipes. Thank you so much.*

> *Love,*
> *Marilyn*

Chafing Dish

Dear Donna,

*It's obvious that when you decided to buy us a chafing dish you
were determined to select the most magnificent one of them all.
You certainly succeeded. Thank you for a beautiful gift.*

> *Fondly,*
> *Marilyn*

Chair

Dear Mr. and Mrs. Black,

George and I find your lounging chair so comfortable that we decided the only fair thing to do is to set up a schedule. Monday and Wednesday evenings are reserved for him, and Tuesday and Thursday evenings for me. We've saved the rest of the week for our guests. Our many thanks.

Love,
Marilyn

Check

Dear Mr. and Mrs. Wallace,

I can't tell you how often during our honeymoon we wished we could thank you in person for your check. It enabled us to do much more than just window-shop. We bought so many things which will bring us fond memories of our trip for years to come. Thank you for your thoughtfulness.

Sincerely,
Marilyn Werner

China Place Setting

Dear Susan and Peter,

As you can well imagine, we looked at hundreds of china patterns before we finally decided on one. Therefore, I can honestly tell you that there is no wedding gift we wanted more. We're simply delighted to have the place setting. Thank you for turning our dream into a reality.

> Love,
> Marilyn

Coffeemaker with Timer

Dear Mrs. Harvey,

If there is one thing George is fussy about it's the coffee he drinks; and if there is one thing I'm erratic about, it's the coffee I make. With a coffeemaker like yours, I can now guarantee good coffee every morning and spend extra time cooking a special breakfast in the bargain! I so appreciate your thoughtfulness.

> Sincerely,
> Marilyn

Coffee Urn

Dear Linda and Ed,

Somehow the way coffee is served seems to affect its taste. Your handsome coffee urn will make my mediocre coffee taste good and my good coffee taste excellent. Thank you for providing such peace of mind.

Fondly,
Marilyn

Cookbook

Dear Aunt Mildred,

I was so delighted with your cookbook that I had to write your thank-you note first. While it is obvious that George didn't marry me for my culinary ability, it won't do any harm if I learn some good dishes so he can enjoy a few good meals. Thank you for your kindness.

Affectionately,
Marilyn

Creamer and Sugar Bowl

Dear Mr. and Mrs. Barry,

Thank you both for the lovely creamer and sugar bowl. Now even the weight watchers we know won't be able to resist the sweet temptation. All our thanks.

Sincerely,
Marilyn Werner

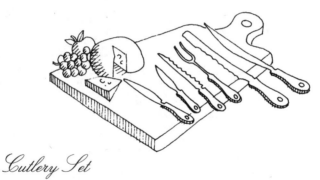

Cutlery Set

Dear Linda and Ed,

Although our friends haven't seen your cutlery set in action yet, that doesn't stop them from commenting on its handsome appearance. George and I join the chorus of praise. Thank you for a splendid gift.

Fondly,
Marilyn

Desk Set

Dear Mr. and Mrs. Silver,

For the past few weeks we have been opening so many gifts of linen, crockery, and "frillery" that George's interest had started to wander. Then along came your handsome desk set. You've selected a gift that appeals so much to both of us. We thank you very much.

Cordially,
Marilyn Werner

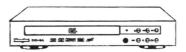

DVD Player

Dear Mr. and Mrs. Rogers,

Words cannot express how thrilled we are with the DVD player. Now that we set it up, we can really appreciate how fabulous it is. The picture and sound quality are excellent—I'm sure we will now become total couch potatoes! Thanks again for such a thoughtful gift.

Love,
Marilyn

Espresso Machine

Dear Joan, Barbara, Mary, and Sue,

I should have known the four of you would have had the thoughtfulness to indulge my fondness for espresso coffee with this beautiful new machine! I can hardly wait for those long, leisurely chats over steamed milk and cinnamon. George and I are just thrilled with your gift. When can you come over and help us discover just the right coffee blend?

All my love,
Marilyn

Fondue Dish

Dear Aunt Betty and Uncle Jim,

Every bride hopes to master at least one exotic recipe. Your fondue dish provides something solid on which I can build my reputation. I hope you'll accept an invitation for fondue and wine when George and I return from our honeymoon.

Love,
Marilyn

Food Processor

Dear Aunt Sorel and Uncle Kurt,

The food processor is marvelous! In two days it's whipped up two malteds, eight flapjacks, and four helpings of mousse. George and I have probably gained ten pounds between us, but who's complaining? We're absolutely delighted with your gift.

Love,
Marilyn

Gift Certificate

Dear Mr. and Mrs. Baldwin,

Thank you so much for your very generous gift certificate. There are so many things I wanted for the apartment, but felt reluctant to buy. Now, I can enjoy shopping, since I know you can't deposit a gift certificate to a bank account.

Affectionately,
Marilyn

Glasses (Highball)

Dear Gloria,

What a present! What a friend! The highball glasses are wonderful, and so are you for giving us this beautiful gift. We lift our glasses in thanks.

Affectionately,
Marilyn

Glasses (Martini)

Dear Helena and Michael,

Even as I write this note, I am undecided what to thank you for first. We can use your graceful stemware to serve martinis, shrimp, sherbet, or even fruit cocktail! Thank you for sending us a gift which has such splendid versatility.

Love,
Marilyn

Glasses (Water)

Dear Sherry and Barry,

Every time I gaze at your water goblets I thank you anew for such a practical and lovely gift. They now have the place of honor on my kitchen shelf, but I really can't wait to set them out on the table.

Love,
Marilyn

Glasses (Wine)

Dear Joan and Fred,

I can't tell you how delighted George and I are with your gift. A set of twelve sparkling crystal glasses! From now on, no more Chianti for us. Glasses like these deserve nothing less than the best Bordeaux or Burgundy. Thank you so much for this most generous expression of your friendship.

Love,
Marilyn

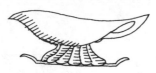

Gravy Boat

Dear Uncle Howard,

It's apparent that you and Tiffany have the same exquisite taste. What a beautiful silver gravy boat! I really have to perfect my skill at gravy making so that only the tastiest sauces are served in this stunning dish.

Love,
Marilyn

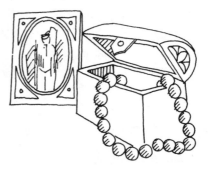

Heirloom

Dear Aunt Ellen,

We feel both proud and honored that you should give us this treasured family heirloom as our wedding gift. Aside from its monetary value, we are well aware of its great sentimental value. Be assured that we will treat it with all the care and reverence it deserves. All our thanks.

Affectionately,
Marilyn

Ice Bucket

Dear Fred,

There are ice buckets and there are ice buckets and they all
hold ice. None, however, holds ice as handsomely as yours. We
predict a sharp increase in the number of our friends who'll call
for their drinks on the rocks.

Thanks very much.

Fondly,
Marilyn

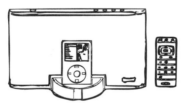

iPod Dock

Dear Mary and Bill,

Although George and I look forward to having toast and coffee
together each morning, we enjoy some music to get us going. Not
only will your gift do the trick, but we can listen to our favorite
tunes on our iPod. What a great way to start our day. Thank
you for this very welcomed gift.

Love,
Marilyn

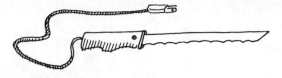

Knife (Electric)

Dear Judy and Bill,

Although George prides himself on his carving ability, the fact is that when he's finished with his furious hacking, the meat invariably looks as if it had just emerged from a grinder. Your electric knife will salvage both my roasts and George's pride. Thank you so much.

Love,
Marilyn

Knives (Steak)

Dear Elaine,

Your steak knives are a blessing. If the butcher mistreats me or if I fail in the kitchen, we can still create the illusion that the steaks are as soft as butter. Thanks for being so farsighted.

Love,
Marilyn

Lamp

Dear Sonny and Harry,

Your lamp certainly does magical things for our apartment. Its handsome shade and base seem to light up our place even when the lamp hasn't been turned on. Our sincerest thanks for such a lovely present.

Affectionately,
Marilyn

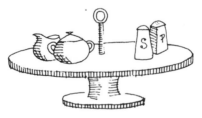

Lazy Susan

Dear Mr. and Mrs. Morgan,

Thank you for making our dinners so much more pleasant. With your practical lazy Susan our guests won't be kept busy passing or reaching for the food—they'll just be enjoying it. We thank you on behalf of ourselves and our guests.

Cordially,
Marilyn Maiden Name

Linen Set

Dear Mr. and Mrs. Day,

Your linen set is the epitome of elegance in bedroom fashion. It's so cheerful and pretty that it even makes the bedspread unnecessary. Thank you for such a lovely gift.

Cordially,
Marilyn Werner

Luggage

Dear Sue,

What a perfect gift! We have not had new luggage since the duffels we used in college. Your luggage set will have us traveling in style. The garment bag, wheeled carry-on, and rolling tote are perfect for our honeymoon travel. With our matching luggage we will actually look like a married couple instead of a couple of college kids.

Love,
Marilyn

Media Center

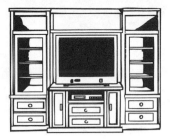

Dear Jane and Paul,

If we put nothing in the media center, your exquisite gift would be the center of attention in our living room. Now, not only do we have a fabulous focal point but we also have a place to house the TV, audio and video equipment, and our extensive CD and DVD collection. We're sure when our friends are over, your gift will compete with whatever we are viewing. We can't thank you enough for this gorgeous problem solver.

Love,
Marilyn

Microwave Oven

Dear Kay,

Leave it to you! This impressively equipped microwave is certainly going to help make our evenings more romantic than antic. With both of us working rather long hours, we prefer to spend as much time together as possible. Thanks for shortening the time we spend in the kitchen and allowing us to cook up more delightful pursuits.

Fondly,
Marilyn

Mixer

Dear Marsha and Richard,

The mixer is a wonderful gift. Thank you for guaranteeing the success of my cake-making endeavors. You can be sure that I won't enter any contests where the rules prohibit contestants from bringing their own equipment.

Love,
Marilyn

Pantry Food

Dear Aunt Marge,

How thoughtful of you to send a gift box filled with items for our pantry. I've been so busy these past few weeks that I'm sure I would have forgotten to stock our cupboards. I can see it now, returning from our honeymoon and attempting to prepare dinner, when, lo and behold, no food. Of course it is just like you to have so much foresight. Thank you so very much.

Love,
Marilyn

Photograph Album

Dear Herbert,

What a lovely photograph album! We're already having problems keeping track of our many snapshots. Your gift will save us from rummaging through drawers and closet shelves in a frustrating search for misplaced pictures. Even if our photos aren't good, they'll look great in this attractive book. Thank you.

Affectionately,
Marilyn

Pillows

Dear Mr. and Mrs. Bing,

It's amazing how attached you can get to something which is so comfortable. Of course, I am referring to your pillows. I am afraid there is only one catch—when we go on a trip, dare we pack the pillows? Thanks for such a thoughtful gift.

Cordially,
Marilyn Werner

Place Mats

Dear Phyllis,

Thank you very much for your beautiful gift. With place mats like these I doubt if I'll ever use a tablecloth again. I can't wait to put them on my dinner table.

Love,
Marilyn

Platter

Dear Aunt Renee and Uncle Gary,

Thank you for the eye-catching platter. Now I am sure that my guests will be distracted from noticing if the roast doesn't come out just right. Your platter is a most handsome decoy and a marvelous serving piece as well.

Fondly,
Marilyn

Porcelain Figurine

Dear Aunt Virginia and Uncle Tom,

Generally we are not a possession-minded couple, but every time we look at the lovely porcelain figurine you gave us we take new delight in knowing it's all ours. Thank you for your generosity.

Fondly,
Marilyn

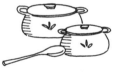

Pots and Pans (Bake-and-Serve)

Dear Janet,

Do I adore your gift! I who hate to wash dishes. Now, with your bake-and-serve ware I can serve with the same utensils I cooked in without having to use any serving dishes. George loves them too—he hates to dry dishes. Your gift makes daily dining almost like eating out. Thank you.

Love,
Marilyn

Pots and Pans (Frying Pan)

Dear Eileen,

At first we thought it was an accessory, then a serving piece, but at last we decided it must be for cooking. It seems all three guesses were right. The marvelous copper frying pan is for all these purposes and more. I am afraid I'll find myself selfishly using it every day rather than saving it for company only.

Love,
Marilyn

Pots and Pans (Nonstick)

Dear Anne,

Thank you for taking the drudgery out of cleaning pots and pans. Your wonderful set of nonstick cookware will free me from scrubbing and scouring chores. This gift makes you our household hero!

Love,
Marilyn

Punch Bowl

Dear Rhoda and Pat,

We don't know yet when we will be giving our first party, but
we do know that your punch bowl will have the place of honor
on the party table. George is busy collecting recipes for a tangy
punch to serve in this most beautiful bowl. Thank you so very
much.

Affectionately,
Marilyn

Restaurant Gift Certificates

Dear Peter,

What a delicious gift. You know how much we love the
Steakhouse. How clever of you to think of getting us gift
certificates. We will enjoy our favorite meals there even more,
knowing it is your special gift to us. We'll be sure to drink a toast
to you.

Love,
Marilyn

Salad Bowl

Dear Mrs. Pike,

Thank you so much for your salad bowl. It is so exquisite that I am considering filling it from time to time with flowers. Using it as a centerpiece will allow my guests to admire it all through dinner and not just during the salad course.

Affectionately,
Marilyn

Salt and Pepper Set

Dear Sherry,

I'll have to remember to underseason my cooking because I know my guests will want an excuse to see if the salt and pepper mills really work. It's a stunning set that adds spice to any table in more ways than one.
    Thanks, thanks.

Love,
Marilyn

Savings Bond

Dear Mr. and Mrs. Oliver,

Thank you so much for the savings bond. As you suggested, we hope someday to use it for our children's education. Until then, it's nice to know that the money is not just lying idle but is helping to keep our country strong.

Cordially,
Marilyn Maiden Name

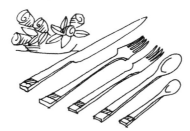

Silver Place Setting

Dear Aunt Mary and Uncle Steve,

Thank you so much for the silver place setting. On our dining room table the set is even more elegant than it seemed in the store. We plan to have you over very soon so that you can enjoy it with us.

Love,
Marilyn

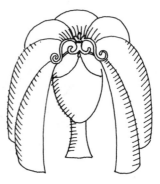

Sleepwear

Dear Miss Lawrence,

Thank you for the gorgeous nightgown. It fits perfectly and the fabric is incredibly soft and luxurious. I really feel beautiful in it. Thank you so much for this lacy dream.

Fondly,
Marilyn

"Something Old"

Dear Mrs. Jenson,

How can I thank you for your tiara! I'm thrilled to use it as my "something old." I've already taken it to my dressmaker so that it can be attached to my wedding veil. You can't imagine how much your generosity has meant to me. Thank you.

Love,
Marilyn

"Something New"

Dear Arlene,

I was hoping you'd be the person to give me my "something new." The gloves are the exact shade of off-white to match my gown. I plan to remove them only long enough for George to put the ring on my finger. Thank you so very, very much.

Love,
Marilyn

"Something Borrowed"

Dear Aunt Joyce,

I was overjoyed this morning when I received your exquisite tulle veil. It is more lovely than any of the new veils I had seen in the stores. The little satin bows scattered around the brim add just the right finishing touch to my gown. I'm looking forward to seeing you at the wedding and kissing you in person for my "something borrowed."

Love,
Marilyn

"Something Blue"

Dear Anita,

How delightful—a blue garter! Of course, it will be my "something blue." Thank you for being so sentimental. Won't you peek in before the ceremony and see it on my leg? Thank you very much.

> Affectionately,
> Marilyn

Soufflé Dish

Dear Janis,

A friend once described the perfect gift as something one wants but is not likely to buy. That homespun definition certainly applies to your soufflé dish. I'm sure it will help make my soufflés soar to dazzling heights. Thank you.

> Fondly,
> Marilyn

Soup Tureen

Dear Mr. and Mrs. Alexander,

*Your soup tureen is so very elegant that it will even make canned
soups taste homemade. When I am asked for my recipe I'll
simply say, "Use one beautiful tureen." Thank you.*

*Sincerely,
Marilyn Werner*

Sporting Equipment

Dear Paula and Marty,

*Were we delighted to receive the tennis rackets! They are so far
superior to our old ones that we will no longer be able to blame
a bad game on the equipment. Perhaps now we'll even stand a
chance against you two pros. Thank you both.*

*Love,
Marilyn*

Stainless Flatware

Dear Mr. and Mrs. Robbins,

Thank you so much for the very elegant stainless flatware. I can visualize guests sitting down to dinner and I can almost hear their oohs and aahs. I'm sure, however, that this will come as no surprise to you, since you obviously selected this handsome set with that very scene in mind. Thank you again.

Love,
Marilyn

Stereo

Dear Mr. and Mrs. Newman,

George and I were so sure that we wanted a stereo that we had a place in our living room reserved for one. I must say we never expected to fill the spot in such a short time nor with such a handsome set. Its sound is simply glorious. Many thanks for your most generous present.

Sincerely,
Marilyn

Stock

Dear Mr. and Mrs. Earl,

Every morning when we read the newspaper to check on the fortunes of IBM we are reminded of your generosity. Of all the wedding presents we received, none is more practical nor more appreciated than our new blue-chip partnership. Thank you.

Love,
Marilyn

Table

Dear Mr. and Mrs. Morgan,

How can we ever thank you! Until we received your end table we thought we would have to settle for a polished orange crate. We hope to have you over soon so you can see how nice it looks in the apartment. Thank you for such a lovely gift.

Fondly,
Marilyn

Tables (Stacking)

Dear Mr. and Mrs. Maynard,

Thank you so much for your stacking tables. The ease with which I can now serve guests will fool everyone into thinking that I am an experienced hostess. I hope you don't mind if I don't reveal that it's really you who deserve the compliments. Many thanks.

Love,
Marilyn Werner

Tablecloth

Dear Mr. and Mrs. Webster,

Thank you for the very beautiful linen tablecloth. The color is perfect, the size just right for our dining room table. It is so lovely that we're debating the occasion at which it will make its debut.

Cordially,
Marilyn Maiden Name

Tea Service (China)

Dear Aunt Florence,

Where did you ever find such an original tea service? Until we opened your gift we thought they all looked alike. Thank you for the most distinctive tea service ever.

Love,
Marilyn

Tea Service (Silver)

Dear Mr. and Mrs. Carlsbad,

A silver tea service! I could hardly believe my eyes. This prized possession is something every bride dreams of owning but resigns herself to doing without for many years. Not only will I display it prominently, but I'll even find polishing it a pleasure. George and I thank you for your magnificent gift.

Love,
Marilyn

Tickets (Football)

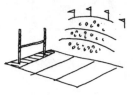

Dear Larry,

We were delightfully surprised to find the season football tickets enclosed in your lovely letter. I adore the sport and George is one of the most enthusiastic fans the game has ever had. The television broadcasts leave out the hot dogs, burgers, and the colorful excitement of being there. Your gift has really scored a touchdown with us. Thank you very much.

> Fondly,
> Marilyn

Tickets (Opera)

Dear Aunt Carol and Uncle Roger,

Thank you so much for the season opera tickets. It's so nice not to have to choose between La Traviata, Carmen, *and* Madame Butterfly—*now we can attend all our favorites. George and I are so glad you can be present for our rendition of the "Wedding March" from Lohengrin next Sunday.

> Love,
> Marilyn

Toaster

Dear Mark,

The legend of the bride burning the morning toast is quite funny—provided you're not the arsonist. Thanks to your ultramodern toaster I can now prepare breakfast with supreme confidence. All my appreciation.

Fondly,
Marilyn

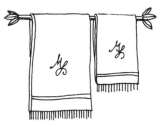

Towels

Dear Gloria,

Your colorful guest towels are a joy to behold. George and I are only afraid that our guests will air-dry their hands rather than soil such an elegant set. Many thanks.

Love,
Marilyn

Tray (Silver)

Dear Mrs. Edwards,

George and I would like to thank you and Mr. Edwards for the magnificent silver tray. I only hope we will be able to stand all the envious glances we get when we use it. Thank you for a marvelous gift.

Affectionately,
Marilyn

TV

Dear Uncle John,

We thought we would have to wait a while to buy the TV we really wanted—and then your gift arrived. The wide flat screen fits perfectly on our living room wall. The picture is so clear we feel like we are in the center of the action. We can't wait to invite you over to watch a movie or a game. Our thanks comes with free popcorn of course.

Love,
Marilyn

Vacuum Cleaner

Dear Mr. and Mrs. Singer,

I consider your gift a lifesaver. My
experience in keeping house is nil, and
yet somehow I will have to succeed. After receiving your
deluxe vacuum cleaner and putting it through a trial run I feel
considerably less anxious about my future performance as a
housekeeper. Your kindness is very much appreciated.

Fondly,
Marilyn

Vase

Dear Rita and Meryl,

What a beautiful vase! We'll have to reserve it for only the very
prettiest flowers, for they are the only ones which your vase will
not outshine. Thank you for a really lovely gift.

Affectionately,
Marilyn

Video or Guest Photography

Dear Aunt Sally and Uncle Jack,

How do I adequately say thank you for your gift of memories?
Your video of the bridal shower and the wedding rehearsal
has preserved some of the best, funniest, and most memorable
moments of our wedding. I can't wait to have everyone over to
see your masterpiece production. Thank you for this special and
cherished gift.

Love,
Marilyn

Waffle Iron

Dear Mr. and Mrs. Powell,

In the past, we had to go all the way to a restaurant for one of
our favorite dishes—waffles. Now, your wonderful waffle iron
has changed the situation. Thank you for making it possible to
satisfy our craving right at home.

Love,
Marilyn

MODEL
THANK-YOU NOTES
FOR SPECIAL SITUATIONS

The nature of the gift or the circumstances in which it is given often create special problems that must be candidly and tactfully handled in your thank-you note. This chapter discusses these special situations with appropriate sample thank-you notes.

The Gift That Must Be Exchanged

Here you must exercise some judgment. If the person whose gift you are returning is not a close friend or relative and is unlikely to visit your home, the simplest thing to do is to thank him for his gift and not mention that you have exchanged it. If, on the other hand, the person is a close friend or relative who will be visiting your home, the best thing to do is to tell him that you have exchanged his gift and why. You should begin by expressing your appreciation for the gift. You should then explain why you have decided to exchange the gift and mention what you have returned it for. Needless to say, your thank-you note should never state or imply any criticism of the taste or judgment of the person who gave you the gift.

> *Dear Diane,*
>
> *Thank you so much for those beautiful crystal decanters. Since we are just setting up our new home, our needs are so very basic that we hope you won't be too disappointed at our exchanging your gift. We truly hate to part with them and only wish we didn't need something so unaesthetic as a vacuum cleaner. We will, however, always remember your beautiful decanters and, of course, your understanding.*
>
> *Love,*
> *Marilyn*

The Gift That Arrives Damaged

GIFTS DIRECTLY FROM THE STORE

If a gift that is shipped from a store arrives damaged, you should notify the store immediately and ask for instructions. Stores usually will send another piece of merchandise to replace the damaged item. In this case there is no need to inform the purchaser that there was any trouble with the gift.

GIFTS SENT FROM HOME

If a gift sent from home was insured, you might write a note like the one that follows.

> *Dear Aunt Sara,*
>
> *How can I ever thank you for such a lovely set of glasses! We've been wanting a set of martini glasses for years. That is why we*

were heartbroken when we noticed two of them arrived broken.
We noted, though, that the package was insured and so we have
informed the post office of the breakage. They will send you
a claim form to fill out and request a bill from you so they can
make restitution. From there on we can arrange to replace them.
Please don't feel upset about the damage. We're grateful that
you had the foresight to insure the package.

> *Love,*
> *Marilyn*

If the gift that arrives damaged has been mailed by the person who bought it and is not insured, you may want to tell a "white lie" and thank the person as if the gift had arrived safely. Otherwise, he might feel obliged to replace the gift and thereby spend more than he intended or can afford.

Gifts from People Who Cannot Attend Wedding

Dear Aunt Edna and Uncle Howard,

George and I were very disappointed to learn that you will not
be able to attend our wedding. Of course, we realize that you
live quite far away. We shall really miss your presence. It was
especially sweet of you to send us a gift of a savings bond even
though you cannot share in the wedding festivities. Thank you
very much.

> *Affectionately,*
> *Marilyn*

Gifts from the Groom's Friends

Dear Max,

Even though we've never met, George has asked me to call you by your first name. Actually I feel quite at ease doing just that. George has told me so much about your joint sales trips that I feel as though I already know you.

Let me thank you, Max, for the beautiful crystal candy dish. I'm afraid I'll have all I can do to keep it filled, since George and I both have a sweet tooth. We are both so happy that you can attend our wedding and that I will finally have a chance to meet you in person.

Fondly,
Marilyn

The Exceptionally Generous Gift

If there is any situation where unabashed enthusiasm is permissible, it is when "a very generous someone" presents you with a silver candelabrum, a five-hundred-dollar savings bond, or a check to cover the expenses of your honeymoon. In thank-you notes for exceptionally generous gifts, bring out the exclamation points and the superlatives. Throw verbal restraint to the winds.

Dear Grandma and Grandpa,

What a marvelous gift! It is the kind of present one could receive only from grandparents like yourselves. Just imagine our excitement, when, as a newly married couple, George and I already have a down payment on a house! This is the most

wonderful surprise. I only wish that I could convey half the
gratitude and joy we feel toward you both.

Love,
Marilyn

Dear Mrs. Jackson,

Yesterday I received the wedding gift of the year, and you and
Mr. Jackson were the very generous senders. I still can't believe
it—nor can my friends (and, believe me, I have told them
all). Three free weeks at the hotel in Bermuda where we will be
honeymooning! At the risk of sounding repetitious, let me give
one last hurrah for your extraordinary gift.

Gratefully,
Marilyn

Dear Harry,

What a farsighted present for a starry-eyed young couple! Your
weekend spa retreat is just what we'll need once we settle down
from all the activities of planning the wedding and setting up
our apartment. The resort sounds fantastic. It will be a weekend
of relaxation and pampering and just being together in a
beautiful environment. Thank you very, very much.

Love,
Marilyn

Dear Uncle David,

When you called to ask me what we wanted for our new home,
I rattled off a list of things. As usual, you picked the most

expensive and the most necessary item—and we really don't deserve it. The sofa is simply beautiful—a perfect shape and so comfortable. All the words we could say on its behalf simply don't do it justice. Thank you, thank you.

Love,
Marilyn

Dear Mr. and Mrs. Peterson,

We are overwhelmed by your generosity! We have put your five-hundred-dollar savings bond in the bank, and someday it will give us a start toward making a down payment on a house or to pay for our children's education or perhaps even to travel abroad. In the meantime, we don't know how to express our gratitude. Once we get established in our new home, we plan to have you over for a gala dinner. Perhaps by then we can find the right words to express our sincerest thanks.

Love,
Marilyn

The Gift from Your Employer or from the Groom's Employer

Don't freeze up because you think that your job or your husband's future depends on your thank-you note. Neither does. Write respectfully but not obsequiously. Your thank-you note should not be too personal. Unless you are on familiar terms with your husband's boss, it is correct to address him as "Mr." even if your husband is on a first name basis with him. Of course, if your husband wishes, he can give his boss a verbal thanks (it certainly wouldn't hurt). However, as with all gifts, the bride is obliged to send the thank-you note.

If the gift is sent by the boss and his wife, address your note to the wife and mention both in the note.

If the gift is sent by the boss and another high-ranking member of the firm, address your note to the former and mention the latter in the note:

> *Dear Mr. Hill,*
>
> *George and I would like to thank you and Mr. Burbage for your thoughtfulness. You must have taken a great deal of time from your busy day to select the silver pitcher. We are indeed delighted to be the recipients of a gift as generous and magnificent as the pitcher. Our pleasure was doubled by your letter with all of its kind wishes for our future together.*
>
> *Sincerely,*
> *Marilyn (Maiden) Married Name*

The Gift from a Group or Organization

The size of the group or organization determines whether or not you write to each individual member. For example, if three or four women at the office chip in to buy you a wedding gift, you should send a thank-you note to each. If, on the other hand, the gift is from a large organization which has dozens of members, you should address the thank-you note to the president or the secretary. You had better pay special attention to this note, as it is likely to be read at some meeting (and recorded in the minutes for all posterity to read) or perhaps displayed on the bulletin board until someone (probably you) remembers to take it down.

Dear Mr. Howell,

George and I so wish we were there in person to thank you and the members of the United Charity Fund for your unique gift. The gold key blank has already been engraved. We shall always remember the key that opened our first apartment door as well as the thoughtfulness of the kind people who presented it to us. I look forward to seeing you when I return. By the way, I think I have a new male volunteer worker for our next charity drive.

Gratefully,
Marilyn (Maiden) Married Name

The Reply to People Who Have Asked You What You Would Like

Dear Mr. and Mrs. Simon,

How very kind and considerate of you to ask me what George and I might need or want. Of course, receiving unexpected gifts is fun, but as newlyweds with a limited budget, we don't always get the things we could really use. We have registered [or, I am enclosing a list of several things] in the bridal shop at Macy's and you may select whatever you wish from the list I left with them. Thank you ever so much for your extraspecial interest.

Gratefully,
Marilyn

The Late Thank-You Note

Sometimes circumstances make it impossible for even the most courteous of brides to write reasonably soon after receiving the gift. If this is the case, late thank-you notes should include an apology for their tardiness and an explanation as to why they were late.

Dear Polly,

Between trying to complete my wedding and honeymoon arrangements, setting up our new apartment, and shopping for some necessities, I have fallen desperately behind in my correspondence. Please forgive my apparent rudeness—I hope you will understand.

Your beautiful serving tray will enable me to be a hostess who enjoys her own parties. Now I won't have to make so many trips back and forth to the kitchen—your tray is so large that enough things will fit on it the first time around. Thank you for the gift and for your patience.

Love,
Marilyn

Dear Jane and Edward,

I find myself in a rather awkward situation. I am embarrassed that you, who have given us such a lovely wedding gift, should receive such a tardy thank-you note. I'm afraid there was so much to do in such a short time that I simply couldn't keep up with it all.

[This letter may be completed with any of the thank-you notes in Chapter II.]

Dear Aunt Martha and Uncle Joe,

We must have started to write you a hundred times but we never could find thanks eloquent enough to match your generous wedding gift. Quite frankly, the appropriate words still escape us. We feel, however, that inadequate thanks at this late date is better than a more perfect thank-you at some future date. To put it quite simply, we adore the candlesticks. Thank you very, very much.

Love,

Marilyn

Dear Rachel and Steve,

I don't know where the time went. It's been a whirlwind of activity for the past six months. There was so much to do that I neglected to write you a thank-you note for the gorgeous cookware you sent us. It's so hard to find a something that goes from oven to table so beautifully, but somehow you managed to do so. I apologize for the lateness of my thanks, but I promise to make it up to you and Steve at our very first family get-together dinner. Your gift takes a lot of pressure off my cooking skills. Thanks to you both, I'm sure no one will notice if my soufflé doesn't rise perfectly since they'll be admiring the cookware.

Love,

Marilyn

Chapter Four

MODEL
THANK-YOU NOTES
FOR SPECIAL PEOPLE

The success of your wedding depends on the cooperation and assistance of many people: the maid or matron of honor, the best man, the ushers, the bridesmaids and, of course, your parents and the minister. There are also your close friends, relatives, and future in-laws who may have given a shower, engagement party, or some other affair in your honor. All these people should be thanked not only in person but in a written note. Here are model thank-you notes for these very special people.

Notes to the Bridal Attendants

Maid or Matron of Honor

> *Dear Connie,*
>
> *This note is to thank you for kindnesses far beyond the call of friendship. I am doubtful that I ever would have gotten myself*

dressed properly without your assistance, quick thinking, and
nimble fingers. Thank you for the loving care you bestowed upon
me. How lucky I am to have a friend like you!

Love,
Marilyn

Best Man

Dear Walter,

We are so indebted to you for so much that we could make a
catalogue of the things you've done, the time you've spent, and
the patience you've shown. Thank you for being not only our best
friend but also our best man.

Love,
Marilyn

Bridesmaids

Dear Barbara,

The only thing that would have given me as much pleasure as
having you as one of my bridesmaids would have been my being
one of yours. Thanks for being such a sweet friend.

Affectionately,
Marilyn

Dear Sherry,

I really don't know what to thank you for first—all the
rehearsals you attended, the various favors you've done for

me, your encouraging words, your friendship, or your being my
bridesmaid. I suppose I just want to thank you for being you.

Love,
Marilyn

Ushers

Dear Harold,

Thank you so much for being such a wonderful usher. Your
presence and assistance meant more to us than this thank-you
note can convey. The occasion simply would not have been the
same without you.

Love,
Marilyn

Dear Stuart,

Thank you so much for all your time and effort. Perhaps the best
way to express our pleasure that you could be one of our ushers
is to tell you how unhappy your absence would have made us.

Love,
Marilyn

Gifts for Bridal Attendants

It is customary that, along with your thank-you notes to the members
of the wedding party, you include a small gift or memento in appreciation of their assistance. You may add to your thank-you note a
sentence similar to the following:

I hope the enclosed token will bring you at least some of the pleasure you have given me by being my. . . .

OR

Please accept the enclosed clock as a small token of our gratitude and appreciation to you for everything.

Parents

Dear Mom and Dad,

Words simply cannot tell you how happy I am—you'd have to see me to believe it. Our honeymoon so far has been a dream trip. We have done nothing but have fun and relax. It almost seems too good to be true.

Often during these past few days George and I have reminisced over our wedding. What a lovely and memorable way it was to start our lives together! What a lucky girl I am to have such a wonderful husband and such grand and loving parents.

Love,
Marilyn

The Minister

Dear Mister* Martin,

So much was happening and I was so excited that I am sure I forgot to thank you properly. I did not forget, however, your

*(or *Rabbi* or *Father*)

memorable sermon and all your good wishes. Thank you so much
for all of your personal attention and guidance.

Sincerely,
Marilyn

Your Mother-in-Law, for a Party

Dear Mother,

I shall long remember that wonderful dinner party [luncheon,
shower] you gave in my honor. I hope that someday I will be
able to give a party that will run as smoothly. It was really a
delightful occasion and I am still savoring the memory. You
have simply been wonderful to me and I can't help thinking how
lucky I am. Thank you.

Love,
Marilyn

The Hostess Who Has Given You a Party

Dear Sue,

If someone were to ask me what friendship is all about, I would
merely cite the shower you gave for me. Your devotion and
friendship were so evident. You put so much effort and loving
attention into the party that it caused me to wonder if I deserved
it. I shall remember your generosity and your party always.
Thank you.

Affectionately,
Marilyn

Dear Aunt Emma,

After your marvelous engagement party for me, I've had at least five offers from friends to trade various and sundry relatives for my aunt Emma. I made the point quite emphatically that my aunt Emma is not available for trade nor even on loan. George is still talking about our aunt Emma and that stupendous party. Thank you so very, very much.

Love,
Marilyn

Grandparents

Dear Grandma and Grandpa,

I'm so lucky to have the most incredibly supportive grandparents. When I first introduced George to you, I was so happy that you accepted him as family. All the things you did to make my wedding a dream event will never be forgotten. Your calming influence meant more to me than I can say. You made me believe that all would turn out as planned—and it did. You've always been there for me—and there really is no adequate thanks for that—just my continuing love.

Marilyn

Wedding Planner

Dear Barbara,

*How lucky we are to have had you guide us through all
the wedding details. Your recommendations proved to be a
perfect match for us. The wedding invitations were unique and
beautiful, the photographers captured just the right moments,
the floral arrangements were magnificent, the DJ had everyone
on the dance floor, and the cake was as gorgeous as it was
delicious. Everything went as planned thanks to you and your
attention to all the details.*

Gratefully,
Marilyn